Russell Carey

Cambridge IGCSE™ and O Level

Literature in English

Workbook

Second edition

CAMBRIDGE
UNIVERSITY PRESS

CAMBRIDGE
UNIVERSITY PRESS

University Printing House, Cambridge CB2 8BS, United Kingdom

One Liberty Plaza, 20th Floor, New York, NY 10006, USA

477 Williamstown Road, Port Melbourne, VIC 3207, Australia

314–321, 3rd Floor, Plot 3, Splendor Forum, Jasola District Centre, New Delhi – 110025, India

79 Anson Road, #06–04/06, Singapore 079906

Cambridge University Press is part of the University of Cambridge.

It furthers the University's mission by disseminating knowledge in the pursuit of education, learning and research at the highest international levels of excellence.

www.cambridge.org
Information on this title: www.cambridge.org/9781108439954

First published 2015
Second edition 2018
20 19 18 17 16 15 14 13 12 11 10 9 8

Printed in Great Britain by CPI Group (UK) Ltd, Croydon CRO 4YY

A catalogue record for this publication is available from the British Library

ISBN 978-1-108-43995-4 Paperback

....

....

Contents

iii

How this workbook can help you

This workbook will help you develop the skills you need to succeed in Cambridge IGCSE™ or O Level Literature in English, or Cambridge IGCSE World Literature. It has been written for use alongside the *Cambridge IGCSE and O Level Literature in English Coursebook Second Edition*.

In this workbook you will find a rich variety of texts. These include poems and extracts from drama and prose fiction texts. Some of the texts in this workbook can also be found in the *Literature in English* coursebook, though the activities are different. You will also find a number of texts that are completely new, and which you may not have come across before.

The activities in this book ask the sorts of questions you need to ask as *you* analyse literary texts. There is a section of study support, with guidance on active learning, essay writing and further reading; then the rest of the workbook is divided into three main sections:

- Responding to poetry
- Responding to prose
- Responding to drama.

All three sections will help you develop and practise the skills you need for exploring and understanding texts – and communicating your responses effectively. Remember that in studying English literature you will make progress over time. If you work conscientiously through the activities in this workbook as well as those in the coursebook, they will help you to acquire the skills you need for success in this subject.

1

Support for your study

Active learning

If you are to get the most out of your English literature course, you need to build your confidence in expressing your personal response to the poems, plays and prose fiction you read.

There is no such thing as a 'model answer' in this subject. It is not your teacher's role to provide you with prepared approaches to answering questions that might be set on the ideas, characters or settings you will encounter in the texts you study.

It is therefore important that you are an *active learner*. Here is a checklist to help you find out just how much of an active learner you are. Tick the column that applies to you.

Do I...?	Always	Sometimes	Never
prepare for lessons by reading ahead from set texts?			
re-read and review after lessons what I have studied in class?			
consult the dictionary – print or online – to look up unfamiliar words?			
make notes as I read?			
annotate copies of poems or pages from longer prose or drama texts?			
research set texts by reading about them on the internet or in library books?			
practise reading poems and extracts from longer texts aloud?			
consider other students' views in order to confirm or challenge my own?			

If you have more ticks in the 'Always' column, well done! If any ticks appear in the 'Sometimes' or 'Never' columns, you should reflect on what you need to do to become a fully active learner.

Key Term

Annotate means to make notes providing brief explanations or comments.

Wider reading log

The more you read, the more you will find reading enjoyable. Over time you will discover hundreds of new words. These will be available to you for the rest of your life and in a very real sense become a part of who you are.

The *Literature in English* coursebook includes lists of texts that are often read by students of your age. Look out for the *Further reading* boxes in the coursebook for good suggestions. Teachers and others may also recommend books for you to read. You can find other ideas in newspapers, magazines and on radio and television.

Use the spaces below as a starting point to list the titles of texts you read outside lessons.

Poems

Poet	Title

Short stories and novels

Writer	Title

Plays

Playwright	Title

Checklist for writing critical essays

Use the following checklist, and the mind map on the next page, to check whether you have considered all the important key points for writing an effective essay.

This checklist, and the mind map, can be used to help you plan and write any formal essays during your English literature course. If you use them regularly, you should become increasingly confident about writing essays.

4

Key Term

Substantiate means provide evidence from the text in order to persuade the reader that your arguments are valid.

Tick	Have I...?	Guidance
	made sure that all my points are focused on the actual question?	Don't write for a question you *wanted* to be set and may have prepared for. Make sure you answer the *actual* question. Leave out material that is not relevant to the question, even if it shows how good your understanding is.
	used paragraphs and connectives to make my argument clear to the reader?	Paragraphs and connectives help you to structure your essays effectively.
	used accurate spelling and punctuation?	Accurate use of English enables the reader to concentrate on the content of your essay without being distracted by errors.
	written in formal English?	Avoid informal English such as contractions (for example, *don't, can't, isn't*). Avoid slang or clichés (for example, *X was the 'elephant in the room'; 'Y was in an unhappy place'*).
	supported my points by using references to the text?	You need to **substantiate** your points by using evidence from the text. Otherwise your views are merely assertions.
	integrated quotations smoothly into my writing?	Quotations should be brief and contain only the word or phrase you wish to comment on as part of your analysis. Short quotations are easier to insert smoothly into the flow of your own writing. Remember always to use quotation marks.
	analysed structure?	In poetry questions and passage-based questions you can explore the structure of the printed poem or passage. In general essays you might be asked to explore aspects of characters, themes or settings at different stages of the text.
	analysed the language?	It is important to comment on the effects for a reader (or audience of a play) of any words or phrases that you quote. This is a key part of literary analysis.
	commented on form?	It needs to be clear from your essays that you are responding to texts written in particular genres: poems, plays or prose fiction.

Engage with relevant detail selected from the text

Answer the question set

Embed many brief quotations smoothly into your writing

Writing a successful critical response to a passage-based or general essay question

Analyse the writer's use of structure and form

Develop an informed personal response

Comment in detail on the effects of the words and phrases chosen by the writer

 **Key Terms**

A **ballad** is a poem (or song) which tells a story, written in simple stanzas, and making use of **refrain**.

A **refrain** is a line or lines that are repeated in poetry (or songs).

Responding to poetry

Exploring the use of sound in poetry

This poem is in the form of a **ballad**.

'O What is That Sound'
by W.H. Auden

O what is that sound which so thrills the ear
    Down in the valley drumming, drumming?
Only the scarlet soldiers, dear,
    The soldiers coming.

O what is that light I see flashing so clear   5
    Over the distance brightly, brightly?
Only the sun on their weapons, dear,
    As they step lightly.

O what are they doing with all that gear,
    What are they doing this morning, this morning?   10
Only their usual manoeuvres, dear,
    Or perhaps a warning.

O why have they left the road down there,
    Why are they suddenly wheeling, wheeling?
Perhaps a change in their orders, dear.   15
    Why are you kneeling?

O haven't they stopped for the doctor's care,
    Haven't they reined their horses, their horses?
Why, they are none of them wounded, dear,
    None of these forces.   20

O is it the parson they want, with white hair,
    Is it the parson, is it, is it?
No, they are passing his gateway, dear,
    Without a visit.

O it must be the farmer who lives so near.   25
    It must be the farmer, so cunning, so cunning?
They have passed the farmyard already, dear,
    And now they are running.

6

O where are you going? Stay with me here!
    Were the vows you swore deceiving, deceiving?   30
No, I promised to love you, dear,
    But I must be leaving.

O it's broken the lock and splintered the door,
    O it's the gate where they're turning, turning;
Their boots are heavy on the floor   35
    And their eyes are burning.

Exploring 'O What is That Sound' by W.H. Auden

1   **Read the poem on your own, and write down the meanings of the words listed below.**

    Look up the meaning of any other words you are not familiar with.

    manoeuvres   _____

    reined   _____

    vows   _____

    deceiving   _____

    splintered   _____

2   **There are two voices in the poem.**

    Working in pairs, discuss who you think the two voices might belong to. Then allocate the lines in the poem to the two speakers.

    With your partner, practise reading the poem aloud, each of you taking the role of one of the speakers.

3   **Working on your own, write a summary of what you think is happening in all the stanzas except the final one. Include a brief comment on the content of each of stanzas 1–8.**

    1 _____

    2 _____

    3 _____

    4 _____

5 _____

6 _____

7 _____

8 _____

4 **What impressions do you form of the speaker of the first two lines in stanzas 1–8? Begin with:**

O what is that sound which o thrills the ear
    Down in the valley drumming, drumming?

Complete your answer in note form in the space below.

_____

_____

_____

_____

5 **What evidence is there in the poem to suggest that the man is a deserter from the army?**

_____

_____

_____

_____

Using the evidence in lines 29–36, what do you think of the man's actions?

_____

_____

_____

_____

6   The use of rhyme and repetition of words and lines are typical of the techniques found in ballads.

a   What effects do you think the poet creates by using the following rhymes?

Lines	Rhyming words	Effect created
14 + 16	wheeling … kneeling	
26 + 28	cunning … running	
34 + 36	turning … burning	

b   Write down one example of a word or line from the poem that is repeated:

_____

Comment on the effect the poet creates by using this repetition.

_____

_____

_____

_____

_____

Extension

1   Search online to find a clip of W.H. Auden reading his poem 'O What is That Sound'.

How does hearing this reading help you to appreciate more fully the meaning and language of the poem?

_____

_____

_____

_____

2   Find an online clip of the opening of the documentary film *Night Mail*, made in 1936. It begins with a reading of Auden's poem of the same name. The film is about the train carrying the post, travelling north across England from London up to Scotland. As you watch the clip, follow a printed copy of the poem, focusing on Auden's use of rhyme and repetition. This is the first stanza:

> This is the Night Mail crossing the border,
> Bringing the cheque and the postal order,
> Letters for the rich, letters for the poor,
> The shop at the corner and the girl next door.
> Pulling up Beattock, a steady climb:
> The gradient's against her, but she's on time.
> Past cotton-grass and moorland boulder
> Shovelling white steam over her shoulder,
> Snorting noisily as she passes
> Silent miles of wind-bent grasses.

Exploring meanings and effects in poetry

The following extract is taken from Coleridge's longest poem, which was a ballad ('rime') telling the story of a mariner. Here the mariner describes the storm and what happens to the albatross, a large sea bird and symbol of good luck to sailors.

Extract from *The Rime of the Ancient Mariner*[1] by Samuel Taylor Coleridge

And now the STORM-BLAST came, and he
Was tyrannous[2] and strong:
He struck with his o'ertaking wings,
And chased us south along.
With sloping masts and dipping prow[3],   5
As who pursued with yell and blow
Still treads the shadow of his foe,
And forward bends his head,
The ship drove fast, loud roared the blast,
And southward aye we fled   10

And now there came both mist and snow,
And it grew wondrous cold:
And ice, mast-high, came floating by,
As green as emerald[4].

And through the drifts the snowy clifts   15
Did send a dismal sheen[5]:
Nor shapes of men nor beasts we ken[6] –
The ice was all between.

The ice was here, the ice was there,
The ice was all around: 20
It cracked and growled, and roared and howled,
Like noises in a swound!

At length did cross an Albatross[7],
Thorough the fog it came;
As it had been a Christian soul,   25
We hailed it in God's name.

It ate the food it ne'er had eat,
And round and round it flew.
The ice did split with a thunder-fit;
The helmsman[8] steered us through!   30

And a good south wind sprung up behind;
The Albatross did follow,

Gustave Doré engraving for *The Rime of the Ancient Mariner*.

1 **mariner** person who navigates a ship
2 **tyrannous** oppressive (unjustly cruel)
3 **prow** front part of a ship
4 **emerald** a gemstone of great value
5 **sheen** reflection of light
6 **ken** saw

7 **Albatross** large sea bird

8 **helmsman** person who steers the ship

11

And every day, for food or play,
Came to the mariners' hollo!

In mist or cloud, on mast or shroud,   35
It perched for vespers nine[9];
Whiles all the night, through fog-smoke white,
Glimmered the white Moon-shine.

'God save thee, ancient Mariner!
From the fi ends, that plague thee thus! –   40
Why look'st thou so?' – With my cross-bow
I shot the ALBATROSS.

9 **vespers nine** early evening

Exploring *The Rime Of the Ancient Mariner* by Samuel Taylor Coleridge

1   Read lines 1–4.

     Why do you think Coleridge uses the word 'tyrannous' to describe the storm?

     _____

     _____

     _____

     _____

2   Read lines 5–18.

     Describe four things you learn about the natural environment.

     ■   _____

     ■   _____

     ■   _____

     ■   _____

3   Read lines 19–22.

     a   Comment on the effect of the repetition in lines 19–20.

          _____

          _____

          _____

          _____

b Comment on the effect of the verbs in line 21.

_____

_____

_____

_____

4 Read lines 27–38.

What impression of the albatross do Coleridge's words create for you?

Use brief quotations to support each point you make.

_____

_____

_____

_____

_____

_____

_____

_____

_____

_____

_____

Exploring meaning and structure

'What lips my lips have kissed, and where, and why'
by Edna St Vincent Millay

What lips my lips have kissed, and where, and why,
I have forgotten, and what arms have lain
Under my head til morning; but the rain
Is full of ghosts tonight, that tap and sigh
Upon the glass and listen for reply,   5
And in my heart there stirs a quiet pain
For unremembered lads* that not again
Will turn to me at midnight with a cry.
Thus in the winter stands the lonely tree,
Nor knows what birds have vanished one by one,   10
Yet knows its boughs more silent than before:
I cannot say what loves have come and gone,
I only know that summer sang in me
A little while, that in me sings no more.

* **lads** young men who went off to fight in the First World War

Exploring 'What lips my lips have kissed, and where, and why' by Edna St Vincent Millay

1   Write down brief meanings of the following words. Use a dictionary to
     help you.

     lain   _____

     stirs   _____

     boughs   _____

2   Write a summary of the content of lines 1–8.

     _____

     _____

     _____

     _____

3   What are your first impressions of the poem's speaker in lines 1-3?

     _____

     _____

     _____

14

Key Terms

Alliteration the repetition of consonant sounds in words which are close together.

Onomatopoeia words which sound like the thing they describe.

4 Read lines 1–8 out loud, and listen to the sounds the words make as you read them.

Use this table to record one example of each of the following sound devices (the first has been completed for you as an example):

Sound device	Example
alliteration	What...where...why (line 1)
repetition	
onomatopoeia	

5 From the table in activity 4 choose two examples. Then write in the spaces below the effects created for the reader by the poet using the sound devices you have chosen.

Effects of example 1

_____

_____

_____

_____

Effects of example 2

_____

_____

_____

_____

Key Term

Sonnet a poem of 14 lines, each having 10 syllables.

6 In Section 5.3 (Unit 5) of the *Literature in English* coursebook, you will find an explanation of the **sonnet** form.

Millay uses the form of the Petrarchan sonnet to organise her ideas. In activity 2 you summarised the content of the **octave** (lines 1–8).

Now look at the **sestet** (lines 9–14). What turning-point in the poem is signalled by the use of the word 'Thus'?

_____

_____

_____

_____

7   What do you think the speaker means in lines 12–14 of the poem?

_____

_____

_____

_____

8   Choose from the poem one example of a rhyme you find particularly memorable, and explain why.

_____

_____

_____

_____

9   Make rough notes to help you answer the following question:

What striking impressions of the speaker does Millay create for you in this sonnet?

Write one paragraph for each of the two sub-headings.

The octave (lines 1–8)

_____

_____

_____

_____

The sestet (lines 9–14)

_____

_____

_____

Exploring language and structure

'To His Coy Mistress'
by Andrew Marvell

1 **coyness** reluctance to do what the man wants

2 **Ganges** river in northern India and Bangladesh

3 **Humber** an estuary in northeastern England

4 **Till the conversion of the Jews** that is, forever

5 **vegetable** able to grow

6 **vault** chamber used for burials

7 **transpires** leaks out

8 **slow-chapped** slowly eating

Had we but world enough, and time,
This coyness[1], Lady, were no crime.
We would sit down, and think which way
To walk, and pass our long love's day.
Thou by the Indian Ganges'[2] side.   5
Shouldst rubies find: I by the tide
Of Humber[3] would complain. I would
Love you ten years before the flood:
And you should, if you please, refuse
Till the conversion of the Jews[4].   10
My vegetable[5] love should grow
Vaster then empires, and more slow.
An hundred years should go to praise
Thine eyes, and on thy forehead gaze.
Two hundred to adore each breast: 15
But thirty thousand to the rest.
An age at least to every part,
And the last age should show your heart:
For, Lady, you deserve this state;
Nor would I love at lower rate.   20

But at my back I always hear
Time's wingèd chariot hurrying near:
And yonder all before us lie
Deserts of vast eternity.
Thy beauty shall no more be found;   25
Nor, in thy marble vault[6], shall sound
My echoing song: then worms shall try
That long-preserved virginity:
And your quaint honour turn to dust;
And into ashes all my lust.   30
The grave's a fine and private place,
But none, I think, do there embrace.

Now, therefore, while the youthful hue
Sits on thy skin like morning dew,
And while thy willing soul transpires[7]   35
At every pore with instant fires,
Now let us sport us while we may;
And now, like amorous birds of prey,
Rather at once our time devour,
Than languish in his slow-chapped[8] power.   40
Let us roll all our strength, and all
Our sweetness, up into one ball:

And tear our pleasures with rough strife,
Thorough the iron gates of life.
Thus, though we cannot make our sun   45
Stand still, yet we will make him run.

Exploring 'To His Coy Mistress' by Andrew Marvell

It is important to be able to identify common literary devices that writers use in order to create specific effects for the readers of their poems, plays and prose fiction. The terms that describe these devices are useful in communicating your personal responses to the texts you read.

An important point to remember about literary terms – don't over-use them! Writing literature essays isn't about dazzling your reader with your use of impressive literary terms. It is important that you use these terms only **as part of** your overall analysis.

You should not simply identify or describe the devices writers use. You will need to:

- explore precisely the effects particular devices create for readers (starting with your own impressions)
- consider how the devices used help to convey meaning.

'To His Coy Mistress' is also featured in Section 6.1 (Unit 6) of the Literature in English *coursebook. The activities that follow should be completed **after** those in the coursebook.*

1   **Some useful literary terms are listed below. Check your understanding of these terms and complete the table with the meaning of each term in your own words.**

Category	Device	What it means
sound devices	alliteration	
	assonance	
	onomatopoeia	
	rhythm	
	rhyme	
imagery	simile	
	metaphor	
	personification	

Category	Device	What it means
rhetorical devices	rhetorical question	
	repetition	
	hyperbole	
	irony	

2   Look at the brief quotations from the poem 'To His Coy Mistress' in the table below.

For each quotation add the name of the device and a brief explanation of the effect created for the reader. Remember your comments on effects should reflect the overall meanings of the poem in which the speaker persuades his 'mistress' that time is passing quickly. See the example provided in the table below.

Quotation	Device and effect created
An hundred years should go to praise / Thine eyes	
Time's wingèd chariot hurrying near	This metaphor powerfully conveys the speed of time passing and is an important aspect of the speaker's argument that they must, therefore, make the most of time.
And yonder all before us lie Deserts of vast eternity	
. . . shall sound My echoing song	
. . . then worms shall try That long preserved virginity	
like amorous birds of prey	
tear our pleasures with rough strife	

Quotation	Device and effect created
Thus, though we cannot make our sun Stand still, yet we will make him run.	

3   When reading poetry, pause at the ends of lines only where there is punctuation, such as a comma or full stop. This is important whether you are reading silently or aloud. It would be a mistake to stop and pause at the end of each line of a poem. Such an approach would get in the way of understanding what the poet has to say.

Working in groups of **three**, practise reading aloud the poem 'To His Coy Mistress'.

Each student should take responsibility for one of the three sections of the poem:

1   lines 1–20

2   lines 21–32

3   lines 33–46

In your readings, adopt a suitable tone of voice for the particular section you are reading.

4   Write your reply to the speaker of the poem.

You may write in verse or prose.

_____

_____

_____

_____

_____

_____

_____

_____

_____

_____

Exploring the effects of imagery

'Blackberry-Picking'
by Seamus Heaney

Late August, given heavy rain and sun
For a full week, the blackberries would ripen.
At first, just one, a glossy purple clot
Among others, red, green, hard as a knot.
You ate that first one and its flesh was sweet   5
Like thickened wine: summer's blood was in it
Leaving stains upon the tongue and lust[1] for
Picking. Then red ones inked up, and that hunger
Sent us out with milk-cans, pea-tins, jam-pots
Where briars scratched and wet grass bleached our boots.   10
Round hayfields, cornfields and potato-drills,
We trekked and picked until the cans were full,
Until the tinkling bottom had been covered
With green ones, and on top big dark blobs burned
Like a plate of eyes. Our hands were peppered   15
With thorn pricks, our palms sticky as Bluebeard's[2].

We hoarded the fresh berries in the byre.
But when the bath was filled we found a fur,
A rat-grey fungus, glutting on our cache.
The juice was stinking too. Once off the bush   20
The fruit fermented, the sweet flesh would turn sour.
I always felt like crying. It wasn't fair
That all the lovely canfuls smelt of rot.
Each year I hoped they'd keep, knew they would not.

1 **lust** strong desire

2 **Bluebeard** a notorious murderer and pirate-type figure

21

This poem is also featured in Section 5.1 (Unit 5) of the Literature in English *coursebook. The activities that follow should be completed **after** those in the coursebook.*

1   **Read the poem carefully and annotate any similes, metaphors and personification.**

      You should:
- use different colours to indicate the three types of imagery
- add brief notes in the space around the poem.

2   Use your highlighting and annotations from activity 1 to answer
    questions a and b below.

    Use brief quotations to support your points.

    Remember to comment on the effects of particular images.

    a   How does Heaney use imagery in the first stanza (lines 1–16) to capture
        the children's excitement?

    _____

    _____

    _____

    _____

    _____

    _____

    _____

    b   How does Heaney use imagery in the second stanza (lines 17–24) to
        capture the speaker's disappointment?

    _____

    _____

    _____

    _____

    _____

    _____

    _____

Writing a critical response

Find and read 'Row' by Carol Ann Duffy in Section 6.2 (Unit 6) of the *Literature in English* coursebook.

1   **Explore the poem using the first two activities in the coursebook.**

2   **Write a critical response to the following question:**

In what ways does the poet vividly convey the experience of quarrelling?

To help you answer this question, consider the sections below.

The thoughts and feelings of the speaker

_____

_____

_____

_____

_____

_____

_____

_____

_____

_____

_____

_____

_____

The sounds and images used to describe the row

_____

_____

_____

_____

_____

_____

_____

_____

The way in which the poem is structured

_____

_____

_____

_____

_____

_____

_____

_____

Responding critically to poetry

'Home After Three Months Away'
by Robert Lowell

Gone now the baby's nurse,
a lioness who ruled the roost
and made the Mother cry.
She used to tie
gobbets[1] of porkrind in bowknots[2] of gauze —   5
three months they hung like soggy toast
on our eight foot magnolia tree,
and helped the English sparrows
weather a Boston winter.

Three months, three months!   10
Is Richard now himself again?
Dimpled with exaltation,
my daughter holds her levee[3] in the tub.
Our noses rub,
each of us pats a stringy lock of hair —   15
they tell me nothing's gone.
Though I am forty-one,
not forty now, the time I put away
was child's play. After thirteen weeks
my child still dabs her cheeks   20
to start me shaving. When
we dress her in her sky-blue corduroy,
she changes to a boy,
and floats my shaving brush
and washcloth in the flush. . . .   25
Dearest, I cannot loiter here
in lather like a polar bear.

Recuperating, I neither spin nor toil.
Three stories[4] down below,
a choreman tends our coffin's length of soil,   30
and seven horizontal tulips blow.
Just twelve months ago,
these flowers were pedigreed
imported Dutchmen; now no one need
distinguish them from weed.   35
Bushed by the late spring snow,
they cannot meet
another year's snowballing enervation.

I keep no rank nor station.
Cured, I am frizzled, stale and small.   40

1 **gobbets** small pieces
2 **bowknots** decorative knots

3 **levee** bath-time

4 **stories** Americanisation of 'storeys'
(floors)

25

Exploring 'Home After Three Months Away' by Robert Lowell

1   Write down concisely the meanings of any words you don't know.

_____

_____

_____

_____

2   Find the following information from the poem:

How old is the speaker at the time of writing the poem? _____

How long has he been away from home? _____

3   Read lines 1–9.

What impressions do you form of the baby's nurse?

Use brief quotations to support your answer.

_____

_____

_____

_____

4   From stanzas 1 and 2 (lines 1–27) what evidence is there that the speaker has been ill and away from home?

_____

_____

_____

_____

5 What does the writing in stanza 2 (lines 10–27) vividly reveal about the relationship between father and daughter?

Use brief quotations to support your answer.

_____

_____

_____

_____

6 What do you think is the significance of the tulips described in stanza 3 (lines 28–38)?

Give reasons for your answer.

_____

_____

_____

_____

7 What do you find effective about the following phrases or lines?

Use a dictionary where necessary.

Dimpled with exaltation

_____

_____

_____

_____

… the time I put away
was child's play.

_____

_____

_____

_____

Dearest, I cannot loiter here
in lather like a polar bear.

_____

_____

_____

_____

Recuperating, I neither spin nor toil.

_____

_____

_____

8 After reading the following two lines from the end of the poem, what are your final impressions of the father?

I keep no rank nor station.
Cured, I am frizzled, stale and small.

_____

_____

_____

_____

_____

'Skipping Without Ropes'
by Jack Mapanje

I will, I will skip without your rope
Since you say I should not, I cannot
Borrow your son's skipping rope to
Exercise my limbs, I will skip without

Your rope as you say, even the lace 5
I want will hang my neck until I die
I will create my own rope, my own
Hope and skip without your rope as

You insist I do not require to stretch
My limbs fixed by these fevers of your 10
Reeking sweat and your prison walls
I will, will skip with my forged hope;

Watch, watch me skip without your
Rope watch me skip with my hope
A-one, a-two, a-three, a-four, a-five 15
I will, a-seven, I do, will skip, a-ten,

Eleven, I will skip without, will skip
Within and skip I do without your
Rope but with my hope; and I will,
Will always skip you dull, will skip 20

Your silly rules, skip your filthy walls,
You weevil pigeon peas, skip your
Scorpions, skip your Excellency Life
Glory; I do, you don't, I can, you can't,

I will, you won't, I see, you don't. I 25
Sweat, you don't, I will, will wipe my
Gluey brow then wipe you at a stroke
I will, will wipe your horrid, stinking,

Vulgar prison rules, will wipe you all
Then hop about, hop about my cell, my 30
Home, the mountains, my globe as your
Sparrow hops about your prison yard

Without your hope, without your rope,
I swear, I will skip without your rope, I
Declare, I will have you take me to your 35
Showers to bathe me where I can resist

This singing child you want to shape me,
I'll fight your rope, your rules, your hope
As your sparrow does under your super-
vision! Guards! Take us for the shower! 40

29

Exploring 'Skipping Without Ropes' by Jack Mapanje

In this poem the poet recalls his time in prison skipping without ropes – where ropes were not allowed.

1   Write a rough plan to answer the following:

    Explore the ways in which the poet powerfully captures the speaker's thoughts and feelings.

2   Then write your answer, using quotations to support your ideas.

_____

_____

_____

_____

_____

_____

_____

_____

_____

_____

_____

_____

_____

_____

Responding to prose

Exploring the way writers describe settings

The following extract is taken from the beginning of George Eliot's novel *The Mill on the Floss*.

Extract from *The Mill on the Floss* by George Eliot

A wide plain, where the broadening Floss[1] hurries on between its green banks to the sea, and the loving tide, rushing to meet it, checks its passage with an impetuous embrace. On this mighty tide the black ships – laden with the fresh-scented fir-planks, with rounded sacks of oil-bearing seed, or with the dark glitter of coal – are borne along to the town of St. Ogg's, which shows its aged, fluted red roofs and the broad gables of its wharves[2] between the low wooded hill and the river-brink, tingeing the water with a soft purple hue under the transient glance of this February sun. Far away on each hand stretch the rich pastures, and the patches of dark earth made ready for the seed of broad-leaved green crops, or touched already with the tint of the tender-bladed autumn-sown corn. There is a remnant still of last year's golden clusters of beehive-ricks rising at intervals beyond the hedgerows; and everywhere the hedgerows are studded with trees; the distant ships seem to be lifting their masts and stretching their red-brown sails close among the branches of the spreading ash. Just by the red-roofed town the tributary[3] Ripple flows with a lively current into the Floss. How lovely the little river is, with its dark changing wavelets! It seems to me like a living companion while I wander along the bank, and listen to its low, placid voice, as to the voice of one who is deaf and loving. I remember those large dipping willows. I remember the stone bridge.

And this is Dorlcote Mill. I must stand a minute or two here on the bridge and look at it, though the clouds are threatening, and it is far on in the afternoon. Even in this leafless time of departing February it is pleasant to look at, – perhaps the chill, damp season adds a charm to the trimly kept, comfortable dwelling-house, as old as the elms and chestnuts that shelter it from the northern blast. The stream is brimful now, and lies high in this little withy plantation, and half drowns the grassy fringe of the croft[4] in front of the house. As I look at the full stream, the vivid grass, the delicate bright-green powder softening the outline of the great trunks and branches that gleam from under the bare purple boughs, I am in love with

1 **Floss** River Floss

2 **wharves** places where ships may dock to load or unload cargo

3 **tributary** stream or river flowing into a larger river

4 **croft** fenced area

5

10

15

20

25

30

35

32

moistness, and envy the white ducks that are dipping their heads far into the water here among the withes, unmindful of the awkward appearance they make in the drier world above.

The rush of the water and the booming of the mill bring a   40
dreamy deafness, which seems to heighten the peacefulness of the scene. They are like a great curtain of sound, shutting one out from the world beyond. And now there is the thunder of the huge covered wagon coming home with sacks of grain. That honest wagoner[5] is thinking of his dinner, getting sadly dry in   45
the oven at this late hour; but he will not touch it till he has fed his horses, – the strong, submissive, meek-eyed beasts, who, I fancy, are looking mild reproach at him from between their blinkers, that he should crack his whip at them in that awful manner as if they needed that hint! See how they stretch their   50
shoulders up the slope toward the bridge, with all the more energy because they are so near home. Look at their grand shaggy feet that seem to grasp the firm earth, at the patient strength of their necks, bowed under the heavy collar, at the mighty muscles of their struggling haunches! I should like well   55
to hear them neigh over their hardly earned feed of corn, and see them, with their moist necks freed from the harness, dipping their eager nostrils into the muddy pond. Now they are on the bridge, and down they go again at a swifter pace, and the arch of the covered wagon disappears at the turning behind the trees.   60

Now I can turn my eyes toward the mill again, and watch the unresting wheel sending out its diamond jets of water.

5 **wagoner** person who transports goods by wagon

33

Exploring the opening of *The Mill on the Floss* by George Eliot

1   Using your own words, what is described in the first sentence of the extract?

_____

_____

_____

_____

2   Explain the metaphor of 'impetuous embrace'.

_____

_____

3 In her description of the place, the writer uses words that appeal to our senses.

From paragraph one (lines 1–24), write down examples of each in the table below.

Sense	Example
sight	
hearing	
touch	
smell	

4 Read paragraph one.

How does the writer portray the river as if it were a 'living companion'?

Use quotations and comment on the effects of key words in your answer.

_____

_____

_____

_____

_____

_____

_____

_____

5 In your own words, write down the meaning of the following phrases found throughout the extract:

heighten the peacefulness of the scene (line 41)

_____

strong, submissive, meek-eyed beasts (line 47)

_____

struggling haunches (line 55)

_____

6 Read lines 25–62 (paragraphs 2 and 3).

Using different colours, highlight all the examples you can find of the
following devices:

- alliteration

- onomatopoeia

- metaphor

- personification.

7 Comment on the effectiveness of the following descriptions:

The rush of the water and the booming of the mill bring a dreamy
deafness... (line 40)

_____

_____

_____

_____

the thunder of the huge covered wagon (line 43)

_____

_____

_____

_____

the unresting wheel sending out its diamond jets of water (line 61)

_____

_____

_____

_____

Using quotations

The following examples show how – and how not! – to set out quotations when writing about literary texts.

☒ The writer describes the river as a mighty tide.

This is true, but the quoted phrase should be within quotation marks, as in the following:

☑ The writer describes the river as 'a mighty tide'.

☒ The description of the river is a pleasant one 'low, placid voice'.

The opinion expressed is a reasonable one as the 'voice' is described as 'placid', meaning 'calm'.

But the quotation is just dropped into the sentence. There is no attempt to link the comment to the quotation. The following makes the link more clear:

☑ The description of the river is a pleasant one. The narrator describes it as having 'a low, placid voice'.

☒ The writer thinks the river is lovely: 'How lovely the little river is, with its dark changing wavelets! It seems to me like a living companion while I wander along the bank, and listen to its low, placid voice, as to the voice of one who is deaf and loving'.

The point about the river being described as 'lovely' is accurate, but the quotation is far too long. It would be better to comment separately on some of the key words, as in the following example:

☑ The writer describes the river as 'lovely' and 'a living companion', commenting on the pleasant sound of its 'low, placid voice'.

Exploring prose fiction

The following extract describes a fire in a Victorian mill and people's reactions to the fire.

Extract from *Mary Barton* by Elizabeth Gaskell

'Carsons' mill! Ay, there is a mill on fire somewhere, sure enough by the light, and it will be a rare blaze, for there's not a drop o' water to be got. And much Carsons will care, for they're well insured, and the machines are a' th' oud-fashioned[1] kind. See if they don't think it a fine thing for themselves. They'll not thank them as tries to put it out.' 5

He gave way for the impatient girls to pass. Guided by the ruddy light more than by any exact knowledge of the streets that led to the mill, they scampered along with bent heads, facing the terrible east wind as best they might. 10

Carsons' mill ran lengthways from east to west. Along it went one of the oldest thoroughfares in Manchester. Indeed, all that

1 **oud-fashioned** old-fashioned

36

part of the town was comparatively old; it was there that the
first cotton mills were built, and the crowded alleys and back
streets of the neighbourhood made a fire there particularly to be   15
dreaded. The staircase of the mill ascended from the entrance at
the western end, which faced into a wide, dingy-looking street,
consisting principally of public-houses, pawnbrokers' shops,
rag and bone warehouses, and dirty provision shops. The other,
the east end of the factory, fronted into a very narrow back   20
street, not twenty feet wide, and miserably lighted and paved.
Right against this end of the factory were the gable ends of
the last house in the principal street – a house which from its
size, its handsome stone facings, and the attempt at ornament
in the front, had probably been once a gentleman's house; but   25
now the light which streamed from its enlarged front windows
made clear the interior of the splendidly fitted-up room, with
its painted walls, its pillared recesses, its gilded and gorgeous
fittings-up, its miserable squalid inmates. It was a gin palace.

Mary almost wished herself away, so fearful (as Margaret had   30
said) was the sight when they joined the crowd assembled to
witness the fire. There was a murmur of many voices whenever
the roaring of the flames ceased for an instant. It was easy to
perceive the mass were deeply interested.

'What do they say?' asked Margaret of a neighbour in the crowd,   35
as she caught a few words clear and distinct from the general
murmur.

'There never is any one in the mill, surely!' exclaimed Mary, as
the sea of upward-turned faces moved with one accord to the
eastern end, looking into Dunham Street, the narrow back lane   40
already mentioned.

The western end of the mill, whither[2] the raging flames were driven
by the wind, was crowned and turreted with triumphant fire.
It sent forth its infernal tongues from every window hole,
licking the black walls with amorous fierceness; it was swayed   45
or fell before the mighty gale, only to rise higher and yet higher,
to ravage and roar yet more wildly. This part of the roof fell in
with an astounding crash, while the crowd struggled more and
more to press into Dunham Street, for what were magnificent
terrible flames – what were falling timbers or tottering walls, in   50
comparison with human life?

There, where the devouring flames had been repelled by the
yet more powerful wind, but where yet black smoke gushed
out from every aperture – there, at one of the windows on the
fourth story, or rather a doorway where a crane was fixed to   55

2 **whither** where

hoist up goods, might occasionally be seen, when the thick gusts of smoke cleared partially away for an instant, the imploring figures of two men. They had remained after the rest of the workmen for some reason or other, and, owing to the wind having driven the fire in the opposite direction, had perceived no sight or sound of alarm, till long after (if anything could be called long in that throng of terrors which passed by in less than half-an-hour) the fire had consumed the old wooden staircase at the other end of the building. I am not sure whether it was not the first sound of the rushing crowd below that made them fully aware of their awful position.

'Where are the engines?' asked Margaret of her neighbour.

'They're coming, no doubt; but bless you, I think it's bare ten minutes since we first found out th' fire; it rages so wi' this wind, and all so dry-like.'

'Is no one gone for a ladder?' gasped Mary, as the men were perceptibly, though not audibly, praying the great multitude below for help.

'Ay, Wilson's son and another man were off like a shot, well-nigh[3] five minutes ago. But th' masons, and slaters, and such like, have left their work, and locked up the yards.'

Wilson, then, was that man whose figure loomed out against the ever-increasing dull hot light behind, whenever the smoke was clear – was that George Wilson? Mary sickened with terror. She knew he worked for Carsons; but at first she had had no idea that any lives were in danger; and since she had become aware of this, the heated air, the roaring flames, the dizzy light, and the agitated and murmuring crowd, had bewildered her thoughts.

'Oh! let us go home, Margaret; I cannot stay.'

60

65

70

75

80

3 **well-nigh** nearly

Exploring the extract from *Mary Barton* by Elizabeth Gaskell

1 Write down concisely the meanings of the words in this table. Use a dictionary to help you.

Word	Meaning
insured	
pawnbroker	
gable	
gilded	
squalid	
infernal	
amorous	
multitude	
agitated	

2 Write a short paragraph to describe what happens in the extract.

_____

_____

_____

_____

3 Read lines 11–29.

Write down in your own words what you learn about the area surrounding the mill.

_____

_____

_____

_____

_____

4 Read again the parts of the extract in which Mary appears.

a Describe her reactions to what is happening in the factory.

_____

_____

_____

_____

_____

b How does the direct speech the writer gives to Margaret and Mary (in lines 35–84) add to the suspense of the extract?

_____

_____

_____

_____

_____

5 Think carefully about the effects the writer creates by using the phrases listed in the table below.

Use the second column to make concise notes about these effects.

Phrase	Effect
'a murmur of many voices whenever the roaring of the flames ceased'	
'upward-turned faces moved with one accord'	
'sent forth its infernal tongues from every window hole, licking the black walls with amorous fierceness'	
'the heated air, the roaring flames, the dizzy light, and the agitated and murmuring crowd, had bewildered her thoughts'	

6 Choose one of the phrases in activity 5.

In sentences, write about the effects created by the writer's use of particular words.

Use quotations to support your points.

_____

_____

_____

_____

_____

Link

Read again the advice on using quotations on page 36.

7 Look again at this description of a gin palace:

'…the splendidly fitted-up room, with its painted walls, its pillared recesses, its gilded and gorgeous fittings-up, its miserable squalid inmates'.

Comment on the words used to make the contrast between the setting and the people in it.

How writers present their characters

In this extract Mama and Papa are working hard at arranging a marriage for their daughter Uma.

Extract from *Fasting, Feasting* by Anita Desai

1 **matrimonial** wedding

Mama worked hard at trying to dispose of Uma, sent her photograph around to everyone who advertised in the matrimonial[1] columns of the Sunday papers, but it was always returned with the comment 'We are looking for someone taller/ fairer/more educated, for Sunju/ Pinku/ Dimpu, even though the [5] photograph had been carefully touched up by local photographer, giving Uma pink cheeks and almost-blue eyes as she perched on a velvet stool before a cardboard balustrade in his studio.

2 **pharmaceutical business** business of producing and selling medicines

The man who finally approved of it and considered it good enough for him was not so young; 'he was married before,' his [10] relatives wrote candidly, 'but he has no issue.' He was 'in the pharmaceutical business[2], earning decent income', which was taken to mean that he was a travelling salesman who received a commission in addition to his salary. 'He is a good family man with a sense of responsibility,' they wrote, which was interpreted [15] to mean he was living with his parents in an extended family. Since it was clear Uma was not going to receive another offer no matter what a good job the photographer had done with his unpromising material, Mama and Papa decided to proceed with the negotiations. The dowry[3] offered by Papa, although modest [20] since he had already thrown one away – as he never stopped reminding the women in the family – must have seemed like a bonus to a man who may not have expected more than one dowry in a lifetime. It was accepted with alacrity.

3 **dowry** cash or gifts offered to the bridegroom's family from the bride's family

Since the previous meeting between the prospective bride and [25] groom had proved so unpropitious, it was tacitly decided to do without one in this case. And so the bridegroom's party was on its way. Mama frantically supervised the cooking of meals and making of sweets for three days in a row. Papa was seeing to the marquee being set up on the lawn, the priest and [30] all his requirements in the way of ceremony and ritual, and the musicians to play during the reception. Uma found herself richer by a dozen saris, a set of gold jewellery and another of pearls, then was handed a garland and posted at the entrance to the marquee to wait for the bridegroom. [35]

4 **rickshaw** passenger cart pulled or pedalled by one person

He came from his town by train along with his brothers, cousins, father and other male relatives. At the railway station they got into taxis and auto rickshaws[4] and arrived at the head of the street where they were met by a brass band and the horse they had hired, a rather spindly and knock-kneed one but [40]

42

5 **'Colonel Bogey'** a popular
marching tune

6 **Aruna** Uma's sister

brightly dressed in garlands and tinsel. This he mounted, with
help from his brothers and friends, and so proceeded to their
gate, his friends dancing and turning somersaults the whole
length of the street while the band played 'Colonel Bogey'[5].

Uma felt the drum and the trumpet sound in the very depths   45
of her chest, pounding on it as if it were a tin pan. Her henna-
painted hands – holding the garland – trembled. Mama stood
behind her, securing the jasmines in her hair, and Aruna[6]
danced from one foot to the other, her lips stained red with the
lipstick she had been allowed to use at last, and cried, 'Uma, he   50
is coming! He is coming!'

He slid off the horse, making it crash its knees together and nearly
fall, then approached Uma with a damp and wilting garland. His
hands, too, shook a little. His brothers, who supported him on
each side, steered him towards Uma, then raised the curtain of   55
silver and gold tinsel from his face. He looked at Uma glumly and
without much interest. What he saw did not seem to make him
change his attitude. He handed over his garland, and Uma was
made to drape hers over his head. She bit her lips as she did so,
he seemed so reluctant to accept it. The man looked as old to her   60
as Papa, nearly, and was grossly overweight too, while his face
was pockmarked. None of this disturbed her as much, however, as
did his sullen expression. He so resembled all the other men who
had ever looked her way – they had all been reduced to precisely
this state of unenthusiasm – that she relinquished all her foolishly 65
unrealistic hopes.

Exploring the extract from *Fasting, Feasting* by Anita Desai

1   In your own words, give the meanings of the following phrases:

'Mama worked hard at trying to dispose of Uma…' (line 1)

_____

'a good job the photographer had done with unpromising material'(line 18)

_____

'It was accepted with alacrity.' (line 24)

_____

'reduced precisely to this state of unenthusiasm' (line 64)

_____

43

2   What impressions do you form of the wedding preparations?

Use brief quotations to support your answer.

_____

_____

_____

_____

_____

_____

_____

3   The extract gives you plenty of information about the appearance of
both Uma and the prospective groom – what they look like and who
they are.

List below the information the writer gives us.

Uma   The prospective bridegroom

4 Highlight the parts of the extract where you feel sorry for Uma.

Then on this page write your answer to the question:

In what ways does Desai make you feel sorry for Uma?

You should:

- use brief quotations to support your points
- comment on the effects of particular words and phrases Desai uses.

_____

_____

_____

_____

_____

_____

_____

_____

_____

_____

_____

_____

_____

_____

_____

Exploring characters in novels

At the start of this extract by James Joyce, the prefect of studies is about to enter the classroom in which Stephen Dedalus is a pupil.

Extract from *A Portrait of the Artist as a Young Man*
by James Joyce

The door opened quietly and closed. A quick whisper ran through the class: the prefect of studies. There was an instant of dead silence and then the loud crack of a pandybat[1] on the last desk. Stephen's heart leapt up in fear.

— Any boys want flogging here, Father Arnall? cried the prefect   5
of studies. Any lazy idle loafers that want flogging in this class?

He came to the middle of the class and saw Fleming on his knees.

— Hoho! he cried. Who is this boy? Why is he on his knees? What is your name, boy?

— Fleming, sir.   10

— Hoho, Fleming! An idler of course. I can see it in your eye. Why is he on his knees, Father Arnall?

— He wrote a bad Latin theme, Father Arnall said, and he missed all the questions in grammar.

— Of course he did! cried the prefect of studies, of course he   15
did! A born idler! I can see it in the corner of his eye.

He banged his pandybat down on the desk and cried:

— Up, Fleming! Up, my boy!

Fleming stood up slowly.

— Hold out! cried the prefect of studies.   20

Fleming held out his hand. The pandybat came down on it with a loud smacking sound: one, two, three, four, five, six.

— Other hand!

The pandybat came down again in six loud quick smacks.

— Kneel down! cried the prefect of studies.   25

Fleming knelt down squeezing his hands under his armpits, his face contorted with pain; but Stephen knew how hard his hands were because Fleming was always rubbing rosin into them. But

1 **pandybat** a leather strap used for corporal punishment

perhaps he was in great pain for the noise of the pandybat was terrible. Stephen's heart was beating and fluttering. 30

— At your work, all of you! shouted the prefect of studies. We want no lazy idle loafers here, lazy idle little schemers. At your work, I tell you. Father Dolan will be in to see you every day. Father Dolan will be in tomorrow.

He poked one of the boys in the side with the pandybat, saying: 35

— You, boy! When will Father Dolan be in again?

— Tomorrow, sir, said Tom Furlong's voice.

— Tomorrow and tomorrow and tomorrow, said the prefect of studies. Make up your minds for that. Every day Father Dolan. Write away. You, boy, who are you? 40

Stephen's heart jumped suddenly.

— Dedalus, sir.

— Why are you not writing like the others?

— I ... my ...

He could not speak with fright. 45

— Why is he not writing, Father Arnall?

2 **exempted** released

— He broke his glasses, said Father Arnall, and I exempted[2] him from work.

— Broke? What is this I hear? What is this your name is? said the prefect of studies. 50

— Dedalus, sir.

— Out here, Dedalus. Lazy little schemer. I see schemer in your face. Where did you break your glasses?

Stephen stumbled into the middle of the class, blinded by fear and haste. 55

— Where did you break your glasses? repeated the prefect of studies.

— The cinderpath, sir.

— Hoho! The cinderpath! cried the prefect of studies. I know that trick. 60

Stephen lifted his eyes in wonder and saw for a moment Father Dolan's white-grey not young face, his baldy white-grey head with fluff at the sides of it, the steel rims of his spectacles

and his no-coloured eyes looking through the glasses. Why did
he say that he knew that trick? 65

— Lazy idle little loafer! cried the prefect of studies. Broke my
glasses! An old schoolboy trick! Out with your hand this moment!

Stephen closed his eyes and held out in the air his trembling
hand with the palm upwards. He felt the prefect of studies touch
it for a moment at the fingers to straighten it and then the swish of 70
the sleeve of the soutane[3] as the pandybat was lifted to strike. A hot
burning stinging tingling blow like the loud crack of a broken stick
made his trembling hand crumple together like a leaf in the fire:
and at the sound and the pain scalding tears were driven into his
eyes. His whole body was shaking with fright, his arm was shaking 75
and his crumpled burning livid hand shook like a loose leaf in the
air. A cry sprang to his lips, a prayer to be let off. But though the
tears scalded his eyes and his limbs quivered with pain and fright
he held back the hot tears and the cry that scalded his throat.

— Other hand! shouted the prefect of studies. 80

Stephen drew back his maimed and quivering right arm and
held out his left hand. The soutane sleeve swished again as the
pandybat was lifted and a loud crashing sound and a fierce
maddening tingling burning pain made his hand shrink together
with the palms and fingers in a livid quivering mass. The scalding 85
water burst forth from his eyes and, burning with shame and agony
and fear, he drew back his shaking arm in terror and burst out into
a whine of pain. His body shook with a palsy of fright and in shame
and rage he felt the scalding cry come from his throat and the
scalding tears falling out of his eyes and down his flaming cheeks. 90

— Kneel down! cried the prefect of studies.

Stephen knelt down quickly pressing his beaten hands to
his sides. To think of them beaten and swollen with pain all in
a moment made him feel so sorry for them as if they were not
his hands but someone else's that he felt sorry for. And as he 95
knelt, calming the last sobs in his throat and feeling the burning
tingling pain pressed into his sides, he thought of the hands
which he had held out in the air with the palms up and of the
firm touch of the prefect of studies when he had steadied the
shaking fingers and of the beaten swollen reddened mass of 100
palm and fingers that shook helplessly in the air.

— Get at your work, all of you, cried the prefect of studies from
the door. Father Dolan will be in every day to see if any boy, any
lazy idle little loafer wants flogging. Every day. Every day.

The door closed behind him. 105

3 **soutane** cassock, item of clothing worn by Christian clergy

48

Exploring the extract from *A Portrait of the Artist as a Young Man* by James Joyce

1   Read lines 1–60.

How do you think James Joyce makes the prefect of studies such a frightening figure?

Note down your points and supporting quotations in the table below.

Point	Supporting quotation

2   Write two paragraphs in which you answer the question:

How do you think James Joyce makes the prefect of studies such a frightening figure?

Remember to:

- integrate quotations effectively
- comment on the effects of key words and phrases.

_____

_____

_____

_____

_____

_____

_____

_____

_____

_____

_____

_____

_____

3 **Read lines 61–105 from 'Stephen lifted his eyes in wonder…'**

Highlight words and phrases where you learn about Stephen's thoughts and feelings. Use the highlighted words and phrases to answer the following question:

In what ways does Joyce vividly capture Stephen's thoughts and feelings in lines 61–105?

Remember to:

- integrate quotations effectively
- comment on the effects of key words and phrases.

Use the space below to plan your answer.

Use the space below to write your answer.

_____

_____

_____

_____

_____

_____

_____

_____

_____

_____

_____

_____

_____

_____

_____

_____

_____

_____

_____

_____

_____

_____

_____

_____

_____

_____

_____

Exploring how writers present relationships

The activities below provide a more structured approach to an 'unseen' passage in the _Literature in English_ coursebook.

Read the extract from _A Suitable Boy_ by Vikram Seth in Section 19.3 (Unit 19) of the coursebook. The passage features the **dialogue** between a mother, Mrs Rupa Mehra, and her daughter Lata.

Key Term

Dialogue the words spoken by characters

1   **Use the spaces below for mind maps or bullet points to plan your responses to the following questions.**

    a   What vivid impressions of the mother does the writer create for you?

b   How does the writer amusingly portray Lata's reactions to her mother?

2   **In your own words, write down the meanings of the following phrases:**

avoided the maternal imperative

_____

at moments of exceptional sentiment

_____

robust, cheerful form

_____

3   **Explore the ways in which the writer makes the conversation in the extract between mother and daughter so amusing.**

Use brief quotations to support your answer and comment on the key words and phrases.

Use the space below to write your answer.

_____

_____

How writers present themes

Read the extract from 'The Young Couple' by Ruth Prawer Jhabvala in Section 9.2 (Unit 9) of the *Literature in English* coursebook.

Then attempt the following activities.

1   **The plot of the story is what happens on the surface of the text. The theme (or themes) of the story refers to what the story is about at a deeper level.**

   Look at the statements below. Which statements relate to the plot of the story? Which statements relate to themes?

   Put a tick in the correct column. The first one has been completed for you.

	Plot	Theme
The story is about tensions within family life.		✓
The young couple move to India to get married.		
The conflict between younger and older generations is at the heart of the story.		
The story concerns a young couple who go to the husband's parents' house to eat on Sundays and festive occasions.		
The story vividly portrays what it is like to be an outsider.		

2   **Towards the end of the extract, we are told that Naraian and his friends discussed one of their favourite topics: 'the tyranny of family domination'.**

   What do you think Naraian might consider as 'the tyranny of family domination'?

   Write your ideas below. An example is given to start you off.

   ▪ Naraian's mother makes lots of comments about his appearance.

   ▪ _____

   ▪ _____

   ▪ _____

   ▪ _____

The importance of openings and endings in prose fiction

Read the complete short story 'The Pieces of Silver' by Karl Sealy in Section 11.1 (Unit 11) of your *Literature in English* coursebook.

Then attempt the following activities, which focus on the effectiveness of both the opening and the ending of the story.

1   Read lines 1–27 of the story and list below the quotations that you could use to answer the following question:

   How does Sealy make this such an engaging introduction to the story?

2   Write your response to the question in activity 1 in the space below.

   You should refer to the following in your answer:

   - the importance of the setting
   - the description of the boys
   - the words and actions used to portray the acting Head
   - how the opening prepares you for what happens later in the story.

   _____

   _____

   _____

   _____

   _____

   _____

   _____

3   Read from line 211 to the end of the extract and list below the
    quotations that you could use to answer the following question:

    How effective do you find the ending to the story?

4   **Write your response to the question in activity 3 in the space that follows.**

    You should refer to the following in your answer:

    ■   the portrayal of Clement and Evelina in the extract
    ■   the contribution of Mr Megahey and his wife to the story
    ■   your feelings about the acting Head
    ■   how the rest of the story leads up to this moment.

A **third person narrator** is often referred to as an omniscient (or all-knowing) narrator. They are able to tell us everything that all characters say, think and do.

1 **infliction** suffering

2 **mortification and chagrin** humiliation and annoyance

3 **controvert** argue against

4 **'Ulysses', 'Ode to the West Wind'** titles of poems

Exploring third person viewpoint

Extract from *The Rainbow* by D. H. Lawrence

So Tom went to school, an unwilling failure from the first. He believed his mother was right in decreeing school for him, but he knew she was only right because she would not acknowledge his constitution. He knew, with a child's deep, instinctive foreknowledge of what is going to happen to him, that he would cut a sorry figure at school. But he took the infliction[1] as inevitable, as if he were guilty of his own nature, as if his being were wrong, and his mother's conception right. If he could have been what he liked, he would have been that which his mother fondly but deludedly hoped he was. He would have been clever, and capable of becoming a gentleman. It was her aspiration for him, therefore he knew it as the true aspiration for any boy. But you can't make a silk purse out of a sow's ear, as he told his mother very early, with regard to himself; much to her mortification and chagrin[2].

When he got to school, he made a violent struggle against his physical inability to study. He sat gripped, making himself pale and ghastly in his effort to concentrate on the book, to take in what he had to learn. But it was no good. If he beat down his first repulsion, and got like a suicide to the stuff, he went very little further. He could not learn deliberately. His mind simply did not work.

In feeling he was developed, sensitive to the atmosphere around him, brutal perhaps, but at the same time delicate, very delicate. So he had a low opinion of himself. He knew his own limitation. He knew that his brain was a slow hopeless good-for-nothing. So he was humble.

But at the same time his feelings were more discriminating than those of most of the boys, and he was confused. He was more sensuously developed, more refined in instinct than they. For their mechanical stupidity he hated them, and suffered cruel contempt for them. But when it came to mental things, then he was at a disadvantage. He was at their mercy. He was a fool. He had not the power to controvert[3] even the most stupid argument, so that he was forced to admit things he did not in the least believe. And having admitted them, he did not know whether he believed them or not; he rather thought he did.

But he loved anyone who could convey enlightenment to him through feeling. He sat betrayed with emotion when the teacher of literature read, in a moving fashion, Tennyson's 'Ulysses', or Shelley's 'Ode to the West Wind'[4]. His lips parted, his eyes filled

5

10

15

20

25

30

35

40

with a strained, almost suffering light. And the teacher read on,
fired by his power over the boy. Tom Brangwen was moved by
this experience beyond all calculation, he almost dreaded it, it was
so deep. But when, almost secretly and shamefully, he came to   45
take the book himself, and began the words 'Oh wild west wind,
thou breath of autumn's being,' the very fact of the print caused a
prickly sensation of repulsion to go over his skin, the blood came
to his face, his heart filled with a bursting passion of rage and
incompetence. He threw the book down and walked over it and   50
went out to the cricket field. And he hated books as if they were
his enemies. He hated them worse than ever he hated any person.

Exploring the extract from *The Rainbow* by D. H. Lawrence

1   Write down in your own words **ten** things you learn about Tom from this
    passage.

    ■ _____

    ■ _____

    ■ _____

    ■ _____

    ■ _____

    ■ _____

    ■ _____

    ■ _____

    ■ _____

    ■ _____

2   Using your own words, write down the meanings of the following
    phrases. Use a dictionary to help you.

    she would not acknowledge his constitution (line 3)

    _____

    a child's deep, instinctive foreknowledge (line 4)

    _____

you can't make a silk purse out of a sow's ear (line 13)

_____

his feelings were more discriminating (line 28)

_____

3 In your own words, what do think the writer means by the following phrases?

got like a suicide to the stuff (line 20)

_____

betrayed with emotion (line 39)

_____

4 What does Lawrence's writing make you feel towards Tom in lines 23–52?

Use the table that follows to record your ideas.

Quotation	Comment on key words

5   Read the Link and Check your progress features about narrative
     viewpoint at the end of Unit 10 in your *Literature in English* coursebook.

     Then, based on the details from the third person description of Tom
     given in this extract, do the following:

     Imagine you are Tom. Write your thoughts about your life at school.

     _____

     _____

     _____

     _____

     _____

     _____

     _____

     _____

     _____

     _____

     _____

     _____

     _____

     _____

     _____

Using mind maps to record your impressions of characters

1 Choose a main character from your prose set text, and then complete the information in the relevant boxes below.

Title of your set text: _____

Name of character: _____

What the character looks like

A very brief summary of the character's actions

What the character says and thinks

What other characters say and think about this character.

2 Choose a different character from your prose set text, and then use the table below to list **ten** key quotations for the character.

The quotations could be taken from:

- your character's thoughts, speech and actions
- what other characters say about them
- (if relevant) what the third-person narrator says about them.

Use the 'comment' column to explore the effects of the key words in your quotations.

Quotation	Comment

Tip

You can use tables like this to revise details about how the writer presents key characters in your prose and drama texts.

Use mind maps to record your ideas about characters and key themes.

Responding to drama

Exploring the ways in which dramatists portray characters

Read the extract from *A Streetcar Named Desire* by Tennessee Williams in Section 15.1 (Unit 15) of the *Literature in English* coursebook. Complete the related activities in the coursebook and then attempt the activities below.

1   **What impressions of Blanche do you get from the words she speaks in this extract?**

Complete the following table.

Words spoken by Blanche	My comments on the effects of the words
Well – if you'll forgive me – he's common!	

2 List in your own words **five** things Blanche does not like about Stanley.

- _____

- _____

- _____

- _____

- _____

3 For the previous two activities you had to read carefully what the character of Blanche says in the extract.

For this activity you will need to read what the **stage directions** tell you about the character of Stanley.

What picture does the writer create of Stanley from the information provided in the stage directions?

_____

_____

_____

_____

_____

_____

_____

Key Term

Stage directions provide information to directors, actors and others involved in bringing a playscript to life on the stage.

Key Term

A **third person narrator** is often referred to as an omniscient (or all-knowing) narrator. They are able to tell us everything that all characters say, think and do.

Transforming drama into prose fiction

1   Re-write lines 1–9 of the extract from *A Streetcar Named Desire* as if it were taken from a novel. Write in the **third person**.

_____

_____

_____

_____

_____

_____

_____

_____

Key Term

The **first person narrator** is an actual character in the novel. All the events of the novel are told from this character's viewpoint. We see events and other characters through their eyes.

2   Re-write lines 38–62 of the extract as if it were taken from a novel. This time write in the **first person** as if you are either Blanche or Stanley.

_____

_____

_____

_____

_____

_____

_____

3   Choose a short extract from a drama set text which you find particularly
     engaging. The extract should contain stage directions as well as
     dialogue.

     In the space below re-write the extract as prose fiction.

     You may use a first person or a third person narrator.

     _____

     _____

     _____

     _____

     _____

     _____

     _____

     _____

     _____

     _____

     _____

     _____

     _____

     _____

     _____

     _____

Shakespeare's portrayal of characters

Read the following extract taken from Shakespeare's *King Lear*. In this extract, the King is about to divide his kingdom into three parts, one for each of his daughters (Gonerill, Regan and Cordelia). First they must express their love for their father.

70

Extract from *King Lear*
by William Shakespeare

LEAR	Meantime we shall express our darker purpose.
	Give me the map there. Know that we have divided
	In three our kingdom, and 'tis our fast intent
	To shake all cares and business from our age,
	Conferring them on younger strengths, while we

5

Unburdend crawl toward death. Our son of Cornwall,
And you, our no less loving son of Albany,
We have this hour a constant will to publish
Our daughters' several dowers, that future strife
May be prevented now. The princes, France and Burgundy,   10
Great rivals in our youngest daughter's love,
Long in our court have made their amorous sojourn,
And here are to be answered. Tell me, my daughters,
(Since now we will divest us both of rule,
Interest of territory, cares of state),   15
Which of you shall we say doth love us most,
That we our largest bounty may extend
Where nature doth with merit challenge? Gonerill,
Our eldest-born, speak first.

GONERILL   Sir, I love you more than words can wield the matter,   20
Dearer than eye-sight, space, and liberty;

Beyond what can be valued, rich or rare,
No less than life, with grace, health, beauty, honour;
As much as child e'er loved, or father found;
A love that makes breath poor, and speech unable;   25
Beyond all manner of so much I love you.

CORDELIA   [*Aside*] What shall Cordelia speak? Love, and be silent.

LEAR   Of all these bounds even from this line, to this,
With shadowy forests and with champains riched,
With plenteous rivers and wide-skirted meads,   30
We make thee lady. To thine and Albany's issue
Be this perpetual. What says our second daughter,
Our dearest Regan, wife of Cornwall?

REGAN   I am made of that self-metal as my sister,
And prize me at her worth. In my true heart   35
I find she names my very deed of love.
Only she comes too short, that I profess
Myself an enemy to all other joys,
Which the most precious square of sense possesses,
And find I am alone felicitate   40
In your dear highness' love.

champains meadows

71

Exploring the extract from *King Lear* by William Shakespeare

1   Look up the following words in the dictionary and write down the correct meanings as used in the extract.

intent _____

constant _____

strife _____

sojourn _____

bounty _____

plenteous _____

Link

Look back to activity 3 on page 20 in the Responding to poetry section, to remind yourself about where you should – and should not – leave a pause at the end of lines when reading poetry or drama in verse.

2   In groups of **four**, practise reading through the extract.

Remember there should be no pause at the end of lines which have no punctuation.

3 Summarise the content of King Lear's speech (lines 1–19).

_____

_____

_____

_____

_____

4 Read lines 20–26. Rewrite these lines in modern English.

You may write in verse or prose.

_____

_____

_____

_____

_____

_____

_____

5 Read lines 20–41.

Compare the ways in which Shakespeare presents the response of the sisters to their father's speech.

Quote some of the words and phrases used and comment on the effects they create.

_____

_____

_____

_____

Exploring structure and language in a drama set text

Choose a longer speech by one of the major characters in the set drama text and then complete the mind map below.

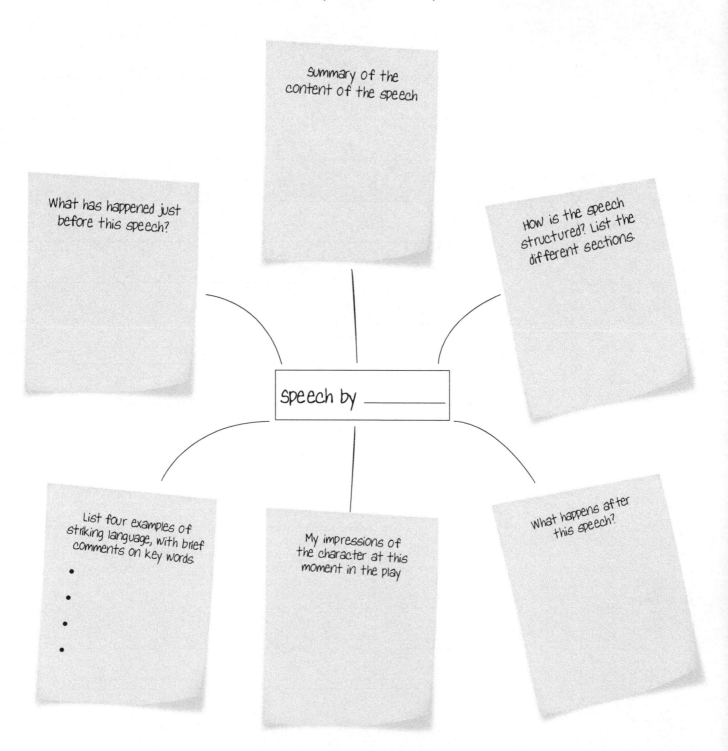

Summary of the content of the speech

What has happened just before this speech?

How is the speech structured? List the different sections.

Speech by _____

List four examples of striking language, with brief comments on key words.

- •
- •
- •
- •

My impressions of the character at this moment in the play

What happens after this speech?

Exploring the opening of Shakespeare's *Julius Caesar*

Extract from *Julius Caesar*
by William Shakespeare

ACT I, Scene I.

Rome. A street.

Enter FLAVIUS, MURELLUS, and certain Commoners

FLAVIUS	Hence! home, you idle creatures, get you home!
	Is this a holiday? What! know you not,
	Being mechanical[1], you ought not walk
	Upon a labouring day without the sign
	Of your profession[2]? Speak, what trade art thou? 5
CARPENTER	Why, sir, a carpenter.
MURELLUS	Where is thy leather apron and thy rule[3]?
	What dost thou with thy best apparel on?
	You, sir, what trade are you?
COBBLER	Truly, sir, in respect of a fine workman, I am but, 10
	as you would say, a cobbler[4].
MURELLUS	But what trade art thou? Answer me directly.
COBBLER	A trade, sir, that I hope I may use with a safe
	conscience, which is indeed, sir, a mender of bad soles.
FLAVIUS	What trade, thou knave[5]? Thou naughty knave, what trade? 15
COBBLER	Nay, I beseech you, sir, be not out with me; yet if you be out, sir,
	I can mend you.
MURELLUS	What meanest thou by that? Mend me, thou saucy fellow!
COBBLER	Why, sir, cobble you.
FLAVIUS	Thou art a cobbler, art thou? 20
COBBLER	Truly, sir, all that I live by is with the awl. I
	meddle with no tradesman's matters, nor women's
	matters; but withal. I am indeed, sir, a surgeon
	to old shoes: when they are in great danger, I

1 **mechanical** a worker

2 **profession** trade

3 **rule** ruler

4 **cobbler** mender of shoes

5 **knave** rascal

75

		recover them. As proper men as ever trod upon	25
6 **neat's leather** cattle hide		neat's leather[6] have gone upon my handiwork.
7 **wherefore** why	FLAVIUS	But wherefore[7] art not in thy shop today?
		Why dost thou lead these men about the streets?

SECOND COMMONER   Truly, sir, to wear out their shoes, to get myself
into more work. But indeed, sir, we make holiday   30
to see Caesar and to rejoice in his triumph.

MURELLUS   Wherefore rejoice? What conquest brings he home?
What tributaries follow him to Rome
To grace in captive bonds his chariot-wheels?
You blocks, you stones, you worse than senseless things!   35
O you hard hearts, you cruel men of Rome,

8 **Pompey** a famous Roman general
Knew you not Pompey[8]? Many a time and oft
Have you climbed up to walls and battlements,
To towers and windows, yea, to chimney-tops,
Your infants in your arms, and there have sat   40

9 **livelong** whole
The livelong[9] day, with patient expectation,
To see great Pompey pass the streets of Rome.
And when you saw his chariot but appear
Have you not made an universal shout,
That Tiber trembled underneath her banks   45

10 **replication** echo
To hear the replication[10] of your sounds
Made in her concave shores?
And do you now put on your best attire?

11 **cull out** pick, choose
And do you now cull out[11] a holiday?

12 **strew** scatter
And do you now strew[12] flowers in his way,   50
That comes in triumph over Pompey's blood?
Be gone!
Run to your houses, fall upon your knees,
Pray to the gods to intermit the plague
That needs must light on[13] this ingratitude.   55

Exploring the opening of *Julius Caesar* by William Shakespeare

1   What do you learn of Flavius's attitude towards the workers when he calls them 'idle creatures' in line 1?

_____

_____

2   Explain briefly the pun in the words 'a mender of bad soles' (line 14).

_____

_____

3 Explain briefly the metaphor 'surgeon to old shoes' (line 23).

_____

_____

4 Read lines 29–31.

What is the reason for the workers not being at work?

_____

_____

5 Complete the following table. Comment on the effects created by the devices listed in the table.

Quotation	Device	Comment
You blocks, you stones… (line 35)	metaphor	
…you cruel men of Rome,/ Knew you not Pompey? (line 36)	rhetorical question	
Tiber trembled underneath her banks (line 45)	personification	
And do you now…? [lines 48, 49 and 50]	repetition	

6 Using your answers in activity 5, answer the following question:

How does Shakespeare powerfully convey Murellus's attitude towards the workers in lines 32–55?

_____

_____

_____

_____

_____

_____

_____

7   List **four** important things you learn about characters or themes from this opening extract from *Julius Caesar*.

- ▪ _____

- ▪ _____

- ▪ _____

- ▪ _____

Exploring the opening of a drama set text

1   Summarise what happens in the first **two** pages of the drama set text.

_____

_____

_____

_____

2   What are your first impressions of **two** of the characters in this opening scene?

Use brief quotations to support your views.

Character 1 _____

My impressions:

_____

_____

_____

_____

Character 2 _____

My impressions:

_____

_____

_____

_____

3   What mood is created in the opening scene of the drama set text?

Use evidence from the scene to support your answer.

_____

_____

_____

_____

_____

_____

4   How effective do you find the opening of the play in preparing you for what happens later?

a   Use this table to record links between the opening and the rest of the play.

What happens in the opening of the play	Links with the rest of the play

b Write a paragraph which answers the question. How effective do you find the opening of the play in preparing you for what happens later? Use quotations to support your answer.

_____

_____

_____

_____

_____

_____

_____

_____

_____

_____

_____

_____

_____

_____

_____

_____

_____

_____

Using mind maps to make notes about themes

Choose a main theme from the drama set text, and then complete the mind map below with the relevant information.

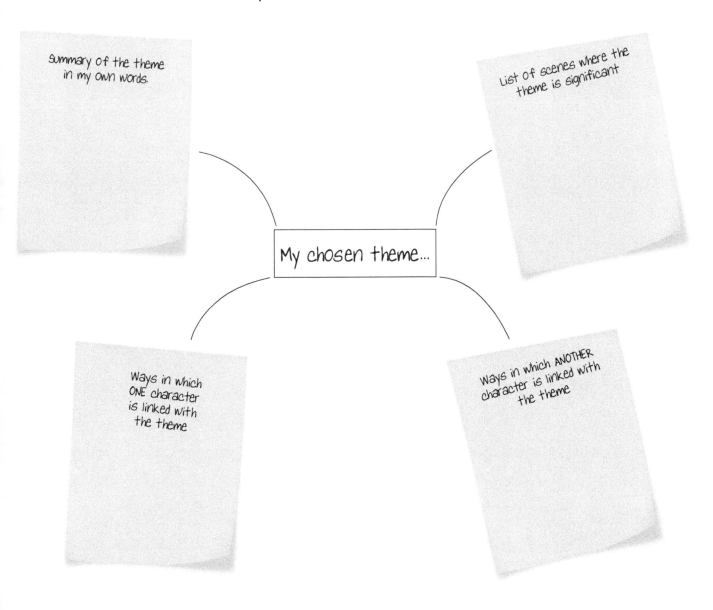

Summary of the theme in my own words.

List of scenes where the theme is significant

My chosen theme...

Ways in which ONE character is linked with the theme

Ways in which ANOTHER character is linked with the theme

Using tables to make notes about the way writers present themes

In the table that follows, add a list of key quotations for your theme and make comments about the effects of the key words in the quotations.

Quotations	Comments

Revising a character from a drama set text

The activities below can be used as a revision exercise for all of the major characters from your set drama text/texts.

For these activities choose **one** character. Make sure you include page references so you can easily find the relevant page again.

1   **What do the stage directions and dialogue reveal about the character's appearance?**

_____

_____

_____

_____

_____

_____

_____

2   **What do the stage directions tell you about the character's personal qualities?**

_____

_____

_____

_____

_____

_____

3   What are your first impressions of the character from their first appearance on stage and from their first lines?

_____

_____

_____

_____

4   Does your view of the character change during the course of the play?

If so, when and how?

_____

_____

_____

_____

5   How does the character contrast with other characters?

_____

_____

_____

_____

_____

_____

_____

6   Comment on any conflict the character has with one or more other characters.

_____

_____

_____

_____

_____

_____

_____

_____

Writing a critical essay on your chosen character

Use your answers to activities 1–6 to help you answer the following question:

In what ways does **the writer** make **this character** so memorable in the play?

Insert the names of your writer and character below:

_In what ways does _____ make _____
so memorable in the play?_

1   List **ten** quotations you could use in your answer and highlight the key words.

    ■ _____

       _____

    ■ _____

       _____

    ■ _____

       _____

    ■ _____

       _____

- _____

  _____

- _____

  _____

- _____

  _____

- _____

  _____

- _____

  _____

- _____

  _____

2   Write your answer to the essay question above.

_____

_____

_____

_____

_____

_____

_____

_____

Acknowledgements

The authors and publishers acknowledge the following sources of copyright material and are grateful for the permissions granted. While every effort has been made, it has not always been possible to identify the sources of all the material used, or to trace all copyright holders. If any omissions are brought to our notice, we will be happy to include the appropriate acknowledgements on reprinting.

'O What Is That Sound' copyright © 1937 and renewed 1965 by W.H. Auden and 'Night Mail' copyright © 1938, renewed 1966 by W.H. Auden from *W. H. AUDEN COLLECTED POEMS* by W. H. Auden, used by permission of Random House, an imprint and division of Penguin Random House LLC, all rights reserved; 'Blackberry Picking' by Seamus Heaney, from *Death of a Naturalist*, published by Faber and Faber Ltd; 'Home After Three Months Away' from *NEW SELECTED POEMS* by Robert Lowell, edited by Katie Peterson, reprinted by permission of Farrar, Straus and Giroux; 'Skipping Without Rope' by Jack Mapanje from *The Last of the Sweet Bananas: New & Selected Poems* (Bloodaxe Books, 2004), reproduced with permission of Bloodaxe Books www.bloodaxebooks. com; Excerpt from *FASTING, FEASTING* by Anita Desai, published by Vintage, 1999, copyright © 1999 by Anita Desai. Reprinted by permission of Houghton Mifflin Harcourt Publishing Company, all rights reserved, and reproduced by permission of the author c/o Rogers, Coleridge & White Ltd., 20 Powis Mews, London W11 1JN

Thanks to the following for permission to reproduce images:

Cover image: John Lund/Getty Images *Inside in order of appearance:* Olivier Le Queinec/Shutterstock; Mary Evans Picture Library/Alamy Stock Photo; Cammiss/Getty images; Silver Screen Collection/Getty Images; Michael Ochs Archives/Getty Images; Donald Cooper/PhotoStage